THEY

Arvis Viguls is a Latvian poet and translator from English, Spanish, Russian, and South Slavic languages. His award-winning work has been translated into more than twenty languages.

Jayde Will is a literary translator. He has translated numerous Latvian, Lithuanian, and Estonian authors into English, with over twenty books to his credit.

They

ARVIS VIGULS

Translated by
JAYDE WILL

Valley Press

First published in 2020 by Valley Press
Woodend, The Crescent, Scarborough, YO11 2PW
www.valleypressuk.com

ISBN 978-1-912436-31-6
Cat. no. VP0151

Copyright © Arvis Viguls 2020
Translation copyright © Jayde Will 2020

The right of Arvis Viguls to be identified as the
author of this work has been asserted in accordance with
the Copyright, Designs and Patents Act 1988.

All rights reserved. No part of this publication may be
reproduced, stored in or introduced into a retrieval system,
or transmitted in any form, by any means (electronic,
mechanical, photocopying, recording or otherwise) without
prior written permission from the rights holders.

A CIP record for this book is available from the British Library.

Publication supported by:

Ministry of Culture of the Republic of Latvia

Contents

The Book   9
A   10
from The End of Summer and Other Poems   14
At the Hairdresser's   16
At the Dentist's   19
from The Lives of Insects   21
September 1st, A Group Portrait   22
Friends   23
Clothes   24
Laundry Day   25
Commentary for Villon's Epitaph, Written for Him and His Friends while Awaiting the Gallows   27
B   29
from The End of Summer and Other Poems   34
Bodybuilders in the Weight Room   37
Brick   39
That girl,   40
Face   42
Mormon Missionaries   43
The Chair   45
Commentary: Shakespeare   47
C   49
from The End of Summer and Other Poems   51
They   54
Home   56
Untitled   57
Morrison Hotel   58
At a Fast Food Restaurant   59
Scenes from a Juvenile Detention Centre   61
Next To   62

Commentary: Mandelstam 64
D 66
from The End of Summer and Other Poems 70
Forgetting 72
Spring 73
Washing Father 74
From a Distance 77
Brother 78
Commentary: Johannes Bobrowski 81
Commentary: July 16th, 2011 82

Acknowledgements

Some of these translations have previously been published in *Mantis*, *The Emma Press Anthology of Love*, *New Baltic Poetry* and *Words Without Borders*.

The Book

One after another I touch my scars,
my only camouflage,
so I can remember who I am.
I don't know how to make the sign of the cross anymore –
this is my last ritual.

The oldest one is on my left shoulder –
from the smallpox vaccine –
round, like someone
put out a cigarette there.
That was my first baptism.

I have many fine scratches
all over my ten fingers –
one for each commandment.
As a kid I liked knives.
In those days there were no other toys.

I used to put all of the
sharp things that you could find at home
in front of me on the table,
and give them names
like they give names to sons.

They determine a horse's age by its teeth,
the age of pains – by their scars.
And yet I'm still very young.
Here – and it must be said with a whisper –
there's still a lot of space left.

A

*_____

The house turns its pockmarked cheek towards us –
an outer wall chewed up by wood-eaters.

The crack in the stone foundation – a lifeline of the dead.

It's like a viper's body pattern, which suddenly flickers in the grass,
or the flash of a camera in a dark room,
when everything becomes visible for a split second.

A shoemaker and his wife. Their heavy features –
anchor cables, which hold the house in place.

He is shorter in stature than his spouse.
While posing for a double portrait, which is now on the wall,
he had to climb up on a stool so he would seem taller.

The wind whips up.
The foliage of the tall trees rustles loudly
like powerful generators.

But inside, in the house, is yet another forest –
a room with stag horns on the wall.
They are filled with some sort of awful extract
like cumin seeds with their own aroma.

A spinning wheel's dry spider in the corner.
Soon there won't be anyone that knows how to use it anymore.
The rusty and broken tools that are nailed to the barn wall,
already having awaited the same fate.

It's similar to those people that are always farthest away in the
    background of a photograph,
no one recognizes anymore.
Faces like illegible handwriting, perhaps in glagolitic script.

You have to practice for a long time so you can read it.
It's just as hard as translating the buzz of insects you've just
    heard in the
grass.

Today we'll work
on this code.

We flip through an old photo album.
A ring with a skull and crossbones travels from finger to finger
for those who are anonymous
like the audience in a cinema during a film,
in which the very same image appears for years on end.

We eat from the their dishes
as if we were their guests,
take sheets from their drawers
and make beds,
which we have rearranged without asking permission.

Meanwhile outside
the twilight makes the colours run together.

In the yard the shadow of a linden tree has ended its path
    around the trunk.
Further away some branches snap –
the underbrush takes a few steps closer.

The forest gropes around to get closer to the house.
It's a strange chronograph with countless indicators,
counting its own darkened time.
(Occasionally deer come right up to the fence.
We're on this side, they're on the other.
We know that animal cages were devised to imprison them,
but we are certain that our cages protect us.)

The twilight makes the colours run together.

The house puts on its modest regalia.
A swarm of insects crown a lit bulb above the porch.
They flicker like scenes in the rays of a projector.

A spinning wheel begins to turn, the film reel gathers momentum.
There's no sound, just an image –
it's extremely bright,
as if reality was too strong for it.

from The End of Summer and Other Poems

I.

Meteorologists and paramedics were still arguing about our
 future –
whether it was going to be hot and painful
or whether it was going to be an ice-cold numbness.

Air masses moved,
caressed by weathermen
on maps in sweltering television studios.

Joy discovered something hidden in us
like a woman's smile that lets you see the small
wrinkles around the corners of her mouth hidden by make-up.

Hope is a distant land – for a few days
we were the salt of the earth –
glittering, coarsely ground.

2.

I put my thumb and forefinger around your wrist
like I was taking measurements.

We were cruel to others, hard from the outside
in order to preserve our sweet softness inside, in us.

We shared one towel
and afterwards
you let your wet hair
dry on its own, without a dryer.

We fell asleep slowly and sweetly
not setting the alarm
as the world remained awake in us,
hard as a pit, a kernel, a centre.

What woke us up in the morning
was a quiet, cautious rain –
more of a caress than a knock at the door

My thumb and forefinger around your wrist –
a warm clock of blood.

At the Hairdresser's

"Very short," I reply.

"This much," she shows me,
taking a tuft of it in her fleshy fingers.

"Won't you regret it later?" she becomes curious.

I've also had longer hair.
At the time the hairdresser
had to hold back her tears while cutting it.
No, today I won't regret anything.
Today it's payback time.

Back then my hair
was long like the swing of a blade,
Now I wanted it short
like snipped green shrieks of grass,
short like a pulse.

In those days my hair smelled like the forest,
today I want
it to smell
like sawdust.

There's only two of us in the hair salon,
which suddenly becomes bigger.

The room expands.

I sit silently
in the centre of her cares.
I won't say a word anymore.

I pay her
for this silence as well.

I think
whether my wife would become jealous
if she saw
how this unknown woman
is working around my hair
with her scissors and comb,
running her fingers through my hair,
softly moaning from her efforts,
so she could move her body around the chair.

While she works with her razor
I feel her breath on my neck
this professional with a faint moustache
and the figure of a market meat seller.
Despite all her efforts,
I am only meat to her.
a sheep being sheared,
a client.

Having reached the end,
she will blow away the fine, black sparks with a hairdryer
from my forehead, nose, ears.

But, as she rubs gel in my hair,
for a brief moment it seems to me
that I am her boy –
an infant in a blue cape,
that she finally undoes and shakes,
shattering this momentary illusion.

"A totally different person!"
she says, proud of what she's done.

Yes I am totally different –
similar to someone,
whose heavy crown is raised from his head
and now he must walk
the cold, rainy streets –
sans a sceptre or umbrella,
free, equal and a nobody
like everyone else.

At the Dentist's

The metal instruments shine on the tray
like a memory of a nightmare.

Gloves on his hands, a mask over his mouth
and he becomes a faceless executor,
an expert on pain.

His needle cheats pain through pain,
but the drill is not sure of it
and does everything so it is sure.

The lamp for the interrogation is right in my face
so that I would confess – the flesh is weak,
it feels.

I spit out blood as a reply.
It is all I dare to say.

My mouth is bound
by a dental impression tray.

Afterwards he carefully records it
in my file.

"I made that
tooth as good as new,"
he says
with the smile of a satisfied creator,
who has already taken off his ritual adornments.

I left without looking back,
hoping to never return.

But time and sugar will have its way,
I will be too weak
and one day I will come crawling back,
calling for mercy, begging,
for his sterile metal
to free me from my pain.

from The Lives of Insects

That book you leafed through with such disdain – about
   entomology – I still haven't given it back to the library,
I can't touch stews with rice, curry, carrots
and corn anymore –
this mixture of colours immediately reminds me of Van Gogh's
   sunflowers,
which are printed on the cover of a notebook in which sensitive
   poems were secretly written down.

I still meet your nephews, brothers, blood brothers –
those agents of the past.
why, after it's all over, aren't our memories erased?

on a city map I draw places with dead-ends,
places of love and hangovers,
institutions where I can't show myself – two universities, one
   library,
streets where I wandered counting the stories of buildings
   – mostly five to six,
a house, in front of which I smoked cigarette after cigarette,
   fighting with my appetite,
not knowing what to expect,

however you were living someplace else for a long time already
and your nails were running through another's hair like
   colourful beetles.

September 1st, A Group Portrait

on their first day of school they look bewildered,
placed in a row like soldiers on the order of the photographer,
squeezed into blouses and little suits that are almost too small,
like they were disassembled and then hastily reassembled again;
their cheeks are tensed either because the sun is shining in their eyes,
or because of the effort of holding the heavy asters and gladioluses,
the magnificent flowers that keep them in the photo with their
    weight –

they are the ones, who sent us memories and bad dreams,
in which we return to our school bench, making up for credits
    after class.
in the dark, when the photo album is left on a high closet shelf,
they, with no one having seen them, fall out, then rearrange
    themselves
without fear or confusion: in the service of memory those called up
know how to reassemble their weapons blindfolded.

there – somewhere in the middle of the second row – is me.

Friends

they speak more quietly, then someone whispers "is there life
   after youth?"
then they fall silent towards morning as the light is grey,
before taking on other colours, standing on the corners of their
   eyes, glass lenses
and the melting stars are clinking in the depths of the glasses

a night, that's spent in a narrow kitchen, breathing through a
   smoked cigarette,
sleeves smeared with ashes (memories of fire rituals?).
and suddenly it's morning. the alcohol is still burning in my
   blood. and it's so quiet
like when a chess player bends over the table at that defining
   moment.

I don't know where their thoughts are wandering to, in some
   snowy Smolensk,
as parched tropes expand in their mouths.
whose turn is it? a hand automatically puts out the cigarette
and pushes a glass a few squares closer to the edge of the table.

Clothes

What happened last night?
Did someone touch me?
How did I get home?
Who ordered a taxi for me?

I went to take a shower after getting up
and a stream of hot water
washed the strange smell that
was not mine down the drain.

The blind pores don't know anything,
their memory is short,
only a blade's cool directness
could pull them out of their amnesia.

What's left?
The smell of tobacco on my skin
a strand of hair caught on my sleeve
a stain on my button-up shirt.

And that will also be wiped out
by the hot bubbly water
aired out by the wind
on a clothes line in the courtyard.

Laundry Day

Clothes are drying on the line in the courtyard.
The clothing of a young family with mamma's jeans and dad's shirts,
and their child's clothes, which will soon become too small.
And the sheets of an old widow and laundry –
as hopeless as lonely heart ads for seniors in those sad, black-and-white newspapers.
And the clothing of young people for a fast life – without buttons and with many pockets,
which were devised only so they would remain empty.

Afterwards the clothes will be brought inside,
the wrinkles and clothespin indentations ironed,
folded and put in the wardrobe.
And the shirts smell fresh,
as if they had never gotten stuck to the skin all sweaty,
the sheets are ironed smooth,
as if no one had made love or tossed and turned from side to side on them, unable to sleep,
and the pillowcases are clean and white,
as if no one had cried into the pillows.

But how often can you wash fabric until it starts to fall apart?
How long is the life of clothing?
How many laundry days will the cotton, the synthentics, and the silk see?
And why on that evening, when the clothesline in the courtyard is left bare,
I have to think –
how many shirts will I wear out, how many socks and pairs of pants,
how many pairs of shoes will I wear out,

until my final laundry day also arrives,
when I will be undressed and washed,
and placed in a heavy wooden wardrobe?

Commentary for Villon's Epitaph, Written for Him and His Friends while Awaiting the Gallows

For those who are hanged
or crucified,
their last privilege is taken away –
to die on the ground,

as if the ground that had carried
their crimes
was not able to bear
their death.

They die like the drowned
who have swum into the depths
and cannot touch
the ground with their feet.

The rest gape at them
like they are gods
or noblemen –
silently and from below.

Those who are hanged –
their throne is the air
and the swarm of flies around their heads –
their crown.

No one can put
a flower or stone
in the place where their hearts
have stopped.

Only their shoes
hang in the emptiness
like strange fruits.
The wind rocks them gently.

B

**
_____

Bushes in ruins from the war stretched out as tall
as boys of that age when they start to fight
and ask why they don't have fathers.
Widows dye their hair which, waiting for their husbands to
    come home,
turned grey before its time.

In the overgrown field, where they once kicked the ball around,
two rocks can still be found laying –
right there where they were once put down as goalposts.

A swimmer springs from a high diving board,
a circle of water closing behind him like the past.

The colours burn like a slow flame.

In the yard a shirt has been fluttering around for two weeks
    already,
with its stretched-out sleeves nailed against a double door.

The poppy seeds of thought blacken in their pods.
The future flops around like a fish someone carries in a net from
    the market,
like a child in a mother.

Someone pounds his pipe against his heel.

A flock of hovering blackbirds weaves a nimble carpet of flight.

Then – far away, the chained-up barks of dogs.

In an open window a voice calls the name of a girl,
and her steps spill out over the pavement.

The older houses of the city remember their difficult childhood.
The steps from upstairs boom in the basements like echoes from bombs.

The wind recounts the plum tree's darkening rosary beads
sunk in a sweet, sticky slumber.

The soiled boys gather in groups like stray dogs.
Their leader wears a wolf's fang, hanging on a dirty lanyard around his neck –
an amulet of hunger.

A public sauna stoker crouches down
to look through the keyhole objective of the women's dressing room.

The twilight weaves patterns in the window like little waves on the water's surface.
When it becomes pitch dark, a mother stands in front of it, lost as to what to do
like a schoolchild in front of a blackboard.

In a shallow mirror hair unfurls over a young girl's shoulder.
The first thorns sprout in her locks, and from morning,
while weaving her braids, her sister will prick her fingers.

The beads, removed from her neck,
curl up in the wooden chest of drawers –
these hard mother-of-pearl berries are this tree's only harvest.

A breeze runs through the room like a bird.
Nimble, invisible.

The shutters are closed to hide memories,
which open up during sleep like an explosion underwater,
like a fist, which knocks on a door for a long time and in vain.

A deep shadow slides across a crack between the floorboards,
where an engagement ring's blind diamond eye rests.

The moon rises – just as big as a clock face on a church tower.
And just as spotted.
Its light is so strong that you can read in it.

In a dream the bloody patch of a poppy field flutters.
Bone logs smoulder.
Between seconds there's no place for a needle to drop.

A cat runs across a town square like a prisoner's look running
    across his interrogator's face.

In an empty classroom a fly sleeps on a globe
right above Caracas.

The night is narrow and transparent like a gauze bandage.

Soon the first light will begin to squeeze through the curtains.
For someone still asleep, it may remind them
of dark blood that seeps through a bandage.
That same sight, just as a negative.

The chimneys compete in height, slowly emerging in the
    morning light.
Beard shavers and coffee grinders awaken.
Colours become visible.

Each moves in their own way,
like on a film strip shown in reverse,
or like on a planet with less gravity.

The sleepy chatter of shutters is heard.

Then the wind whips up like in a metro station when a train approaches.
A bird on a district coat-of-arms, embroidered on a flag above a town council's entrance,
flaps its wings vainly.

The moment a glass slides out of a woman's fingers,
an iron one-legged man, locked up in shackles in the upper tower, throws himself into dance.
It seems the glass shatters from the sound
instead of the impact on the floor.

The winding streets stagger towards a house of worship.

The congregation sits in the pews, each buckled into their own life
like a crash-test dummy in a car that has to be smashed.
In the end there will be a pile of scrap. A pile of metal.

The water here comes from far away.
The bucket dives into the well, deep like a fall in a dream.

The one that has had it will be awakened by the quiet rain.

Frescoes on the wall start to turn
in a flaming zoetrope.

The saints look on. Do they know something more?

The fire gathers strength like a noise from a fan,
as it begins to rotate ever faster.

Afterwards nothing is visible anymore.

from The End of Summer and Other Poems

3.

The fingerprints of summer
haven't yet dried from the skin
like fresh paint.

But still we continue to caress each other.
The fingers remember everything. Those are eyes –
the eyes are the first to forget.

Soon the suntan will begin to fade
and the birthmarks will become so apparent
on the white skin of the swimmers
like bullet holes in the walls of buildings during peacetime.

Little wrinkles, which joy has drawn on their faces,
slowly turn into features,
akin to how a wound turns into a scar.

"This is August," someone says
in another, distant life, which for a moment is heard
like a stranger's steps in the hallway
in a summer cottage, which soon will be left empty.

"This is August,
and in August scars remain
even from the tiniest of wounds."

4.

At night we talked about light years –
us, who count our time
from one beating pulse to the next,
never being quicker than blood.

Time is not seconds or hours
just like an object is not its length or mass.

We talked about light years,
while the electricity meter measured
just how much darkness is in our lives.

In the morning there was only an inch of the abyss left
from all those sharp plunges we experienced in our dreams.

5.

We don't live in the cities we were born in,
and we spend our nights in buildings that were
designed without thinking about us.
Is that why we see ruins in our dreams?

I am like the Northern Forts[1] –
I have a lot of abandoned space,
still the walls have saved a lot of evidence
about those who have been there.

I came from inland,
where houses are built so close to one another,
there's only a thin strip of sky in the window,
where a half-open straight edge razor
is the closest thing to wings you have.

We don't live in the cities we were born in,
we have wandered far from our beginnings,
now we have to blend in with our lives
like a praying mantis blending in with the foliage.

---

[1] Abandoned fortifications in the Latvian port city
of Liepāja originally used for defending the naval
port there. Soldiers would often write the dates their
military service ended on the walls.

Bodybuilders in the Weight Room

The sinews on their flesh form a complex pattern
like fine tattoos
their muscles have grimaces –
their butt cheeks are two faces,
two very sad faces,
that weep salty beads of sweat.

And the blood vessels under their skin
are like a net
they are caught in,
that they won't get out of alive.

And somewhere deep in all of this
is the main muscle – the heart –
a fist-sized athlete,
a pocket-sized gym,
that has to keep this beast fit,
that has to keep it on its feet.

I imagine how after
they've shifted the tonnage of a row
of railroad cars from one shoulder to another,
they all wash themselves together in one shower,
because they have a hard time bending over
and they can't reach behind to wash their backs
because washing such a body
is like washing an eighteen-wheeler.

Afterwards they return home
to their small wives
these small dumbbells of love
bleached blondes or dyed brunettes

that love strength,
with whom they share an epilator
and artificial tanning cream
that give a shine to their cups and medals
and iron their short posing trunks for competition,
because strength and beauty demand sacrifice
and they offer that up.

But at night these enormous, beautiful men
lay down beside them –
lying in bed with a giant like this
is like lying in bed with a brick house,
and it takes all night,
before each floor and brick is caressed
and then they finally fall asleep,
resting their tired, blissful heads
on the hard pillows of their men's muscles.

Brick

It is a creature without a face,
it only has backs – six in total –
that it has turned,
to the north and south,
to the east and west,
to the heavens and the earth.

Too dense to find room in it
for thoughts, memories, doubts,
too heavy to serve as an amulet,
too angular to become a symbol,
too similar to a brick
to be compared to anything else.

The only thing we can get out of a brick
is a wall. The only thing it can utter
is a heavy, malicious thud,
as it falls to the ground.

Somebody knocks on wood three times
so nothing bad happens,
I knock on the brick,
though I know I'm knocking in vain.

That girl,

whom everyone looks back at on the street,
whom everyone wants to buy drinks for at the bar,
whom other women see and pull their men closer to their side –
black flames tattooed on her back above her waist,
a sparkly ring, a shiny lure dangles in her naked navel –
and it's all for nothing,
because that girl will be in despair,
that girl will be alone,
no one will love that girl.

Do you hear me? Sweetie, no one loves tits and asses,
no one loves the bikini line.
No one recognizes your brand of perfume,
bloodhounds are already shaving their heads,
readying for the next hunt,
and all that they smell
is fresh meat.

For them you are only
a honey pie in the last row of the movie theatre,
a sweetheart in the backseat of a car,
a darling in a nightclub toilet for a quickie,
a poster that mechanics put up on the wall in a garage,
so they have something to feast their eyes upon,
before they go home
to their grey, makeup-less wives,
whom they haven't made love to for months,
whom they have fought with to bitter tears,
but who they love unfailingly.

Because we, the fat and boney,
the overweight and bags of bones,
girls with small breasts and big butts,
the pimple-faced, the sweaty,
whose hair is always greasy,
who can't find clothes that fit them –
we are those, whom are truly loved.

Because real love is blind, dear,
real love wears rose-coloured glasses.

Do you see how they look at each other, holding hands,
look how juicily they snog
this girl flat as a board
that guy with tits of fat!
Love has to run through them with supersonic speed,
so they wouldn't care about all of that.

True loves turns a blind eye, sweetie,
but they – all of those men –
they look at you with the eye of a surgeon,
they caress you in the way they caress their touchscreens,
they hold their hand on your knee
in the way they hold their hand on the stick shift in their blaring cars.

Beauty will save the world, sweetie,
but before that beauty will be nailed to the cross
again and again, and again
for our sins, the ugly, the imperfect, the unkept –
for the pimples and dandruff,
for the tires around the stomach and gaps between the teeth,
for the cellulite and bald spots,
for the unshaven bow-legged that are flat-footed,
that stand on the scale every morning
like they're on the edge of a knife.

Face

It has no peace even in sleep –
the whole night the face's roots
work hard underneath the skin
cultivating wrinkles.

Occasionally it tenses up
like it's lifting weights
or trying to move furniture
with the power of thought.

Only rarely does a smile appear during sleep –
trusting and free as a child's
rendering it unrecognizable –
that is my true face.

Mormon Missionaries

A work day from half past six in the morning
till nine-thirty at night,
a contract with the All-Powerful for two years.
They don't drink coffee and tea
don't smoke, don't consume alcohol
and smile so wide that it seems –
their teeth know how to smile by themselves.

These polite prophets in suits,
who make house calls
and always wipe their shoes on the doormat,
the travelling salesmen of mercy,
dealers in holiness,
how did they divide up the territory
with the Jehovah's Witnesses,
potato and vacuum-cleaner salesmen,
and cable TV reps?

During the winter are they hiding
Mormon books of a few calibres under their long coats
like those selling stolen goods hide their watches and gold chains?

Don't they miss home?
Are they wearing underwear
with the stars and stripes on them under their business-like suits?
Or, looking at the sky, are they really thinking about The Lord
or actually about the big, white airplanes,
that have dropped them there –
the paratroopers of the Next Kingdom
with the mission to sabotage our sinful state?

And at night, when God's hand
sweeps them up back to their dorms
like he's sweeping up crumbs from the table
and they, after brushing their teeth, get down on their knees at their beds,
do they pray to That Man whether they could get out of there as fast as possible?
Because spreading the Word in that country is like spreading the Word in hell.
Because we are paying our tithe to the creditors
and no one will forgive us our debts,
as we also can't forgive our debtors,
for no one owes us anything.

Because our souls don't want to be saved,
they're fine as they are, they are like children,
who play with us like matchsticks –
we are those, who must be saved from our souls,
and not the other way around.

Because we don't know how to smile –
our hearts are hard and wicked like coffee beans,
our blood – dark and bitter.
Our winters are precise surgeons,
dressed in white, they drill right down to the bone,
while they lie in the palm of God
like on an operating table.

The Chair

When we moved into
our little one-room apartment,
it was already awaiting us –
an old and creaky Viennese chair
with such naked, narrow shoulders
that you wanted to cover it with a coat,
its legs with bare feet so vulnerable
that you wanted to put wool socks and boots on them.

The charm of any good chair
is hidden in its dignity –
it doesn't fall to its knees in front of its owner,
it doesn't do somersaults,
it doesn't wag its tail.

And what's more –
a rickety and experienced chair like this one
demands a particular mindset –
you have to know how to sit on it,
it is like a capricious horse,
that could throw an unskilled,
inattentive rider to the ground.

I have seen leather easy chairs,
those fat darlings of the home,
which are true bulldogs, bloodhounds,
and business-like office chairs,
superficial and on wheels,
and respectable seats – true thrones,
who even ask to have their backs scratched,
to have their feet kissed,
and the chairs of the open-air cafes,
which are chained to the tables at night.

But this chair was different, this was a free chair.
It had roots like an electric chair.
When I put it in the middle of the room
and sit down,
I feel how the voices and noises
from all five storeys of the house,
all of the sixty apartments in the corpus
flow pleasantly through my spine.

And at that moment I don't care
that I have lived in eight apartments,
but none of them ever belonged to me,
and even this body I am carrying
is rented.
And I don't care that my chair creaks
and wobbles like a calf
that just stood up on its legs,
I don't care that it's boney, starving and hard,
that there aren't any arm rests or upholstery,
because a good and reliable chair
one just like this
is simple and out of wood – like a cross.

Commentary: Shakespeare

Actors found shelter in the countryside –
the plague makes an appearance with shows in London.

The theatre – it's a business
but you can write sonnets for your own pleasure.

Black sparks of handwriting
scratch the paper all over.

Nothingness, a far off land, starting beyond the city's borders.
The dance of death comes back in fashion.

Those who were not yet carried away in a four-legged box,
learn those steps.

So many things are happening on this green pea of a globe.
Pennies roll and fleas jump.

The mouth of the Thames stinks.
A lame dog strives to raise its leg near the gatepost.

Hunger hurls wooden dice
on the dinner table of the poor.

Raising the chamber pot to his nose,
the empire's head physician

examines the royal excrement
and prophesies the monarchy will last for eternity.

The typesetter scratches himself on the printing press
and kicks Gutenberg's infernal machine.

As the hangman yawns, the jokers' language becomes watery
like the soup in an orphanage.

The ships stand in the harbours, having brought
rats and microorganisms.

Australia is still to be found – Terra Australis Incognita,
along with a small planet – Yersinia Pestis.

The pea picks up steam
rolling ever faster around the sun.

But at this moment our hero doesn't notice this,
for he has unwittingly dozed off on the table.

C

***
___

Low-lying blossoms. The colour is like fire
when it is blue.

The village is blurry, as if you saw it in a dream.
or if someone short-sighted looked at it just after taking off his glasses.

The bucket trickles, chained to the well –
a prisoner of the depths.

The wind kicks the cooled firewood into the fire,
the ribbons of smoke come undone,
flutter close to the ground.

The forest surveys its territory
with the steps of a large animal that freezes
upon sensing a human scent.

Further below the river tramples in its own mud.
Mist rises from the floodlands
and wades up the hill.

The window is open.
The landscape, the colours of which are foreign to this area,
lights up, repeating itself on five coffee mugs.
The sixth was shattered.

A mother's hand slides across the forehead of a sleepy child,
which already knows the kind of worries,
that this very palm isn't able to drive off anymore.

Then everything slows down
like the heartbeat of a person at rest as he falls ever deeper into sleep.

from The End of Summer and Other Poems

6.

Ice needs to be at least five centimetres thick
for it to hold a person's weight,
written in a handbook for bird watchers.

I have observed my life,
like someone onstage
who, standing in the spotlight,
tries to make out faces in the audience.

Still I don't know much
about the ground and paths I take my steps on.
We live in buildings, not knowing
who lived in them before us.

When I see the tracks that have been
left on the ground by people, animals, birds,
I don't think about where they're from and where they're going
I think about the rain
that will wash them away.

When the bushes lose their flowers and leaves,
the thorns are still there.
You can reconstruct the past from the things that remain,
I'll track the past by the things that change.

7.

We were close in the darkness
until the click of the light switch
released the evil spirits of great distances.

Our faces could be seen in the reflection
of the bus window
where it was written IN EMERGENCY
BREAK GLASS.

On a piece of recycled paper
that once was our shopping list
someone wrote a short farewell note
before a long journey.

No flights were delayed,
the trains were on time.

Earlier your hand ran through your hair
almost carelessly, almost whimsically,
now it was precise
like an airport worker's gloves,
when he unloads a suspicious suitcase.

Your smile was already the smile of a stewardess
who demonstrates
how to fasten your seatbelt before takeoff.

8.

The birth of animals is gentle
They come into the world with their eyes closed.

I was born with open eyes,
and the light took me by surprise
like a fighter in an arena
who throws a fistful of sand in his opponent's face.

Eyes need time to get used to the darkness,
mine have yet to become familiar with the world.

I have to rely on my touch
Fingers remember everything. The eyes –
the eyes are the first to forget.

They

They will wash their hands before lunch,
after which the waiter will take away their plates and used
    napkins –
dirty and wistful.

His shirt is well ironed,
and his belt sits comfortably on his waist
sure and trustworthy –
he is buckled in well in his life.

She uses potent perfumes with powerful names –
Passion, Desire, Sin,
yet always washes her hands in innocence,
and her face is a stranger –
smooth, there is nothing in it that sticks in your mind.

It's only the eye shadows that keep it in this world.

When they return home,
perhaps only lust will make their well-shaped and cared-for
    features ache
like a cramp makes an athlete's foot ache while running.

But their caresses will be business-like,
it will almost be like a transaction.

Then she will get up from bed, wash off her make-up,
they will take a shower separately,
and each will brush their teeth separately,
with only their spit mingling in the same sink drain.

In that bathroom the sink's drain never gets clogged,
in that apartment the plumbing is new,
in that house the pipes are sturdy,
in that neighbourhood the sewage system is faultless,
in that city the water purification facilities are modern,
reliable, and effective like everything,
that brought them together
in this city,
in this neighbourhood,
in this building,
in this apartment,
on this bed
like a pair of legs,
the knees of which never touch.

Home

The key jiggles in the door.
The dinner table is breaking in half
like a sinking ship out of a film.
With mom on one side, the other – dad.

Each one holds on for dear life
to the plate in front of them.
No, that's not a life preserver.

The chandelier glows in all its brilliance
between the room's Scylla and Charybdis

They have put on their best clothes,
leaving their life vests in the closet.
No one gets up from the table,
until their plate is empty.

The telephone rings.
The Christmas tree decorations
have rolled out on the floor.

A family –
they talk about everything but that at the table
but then the glass balls break under their steps
and cut their feet
as they go towards one another –
right through the pain.

It's the shortest path.

Untitled

…someone else in the corner of the room,
taut as a gymnast on the parallel bars.
heartbeats can be heard ripening.

the knife and question marks have been sharpened.

Morrison Hotel

somewhere water is running in a bathtub, a door is slammed shut,
a semi truck is turning into a parking spot straight out of hell,
and beyond the wall – a middle-aged couple in a newlyweds' room
and next to their door a little angel – a marble imitation –
is rushing somewhere, but is unable to break loose
from its corpulent curves.

it's been two hours and I already know a bit about their love –
a few hopeless phrases from their conversation –
a fight about a needle's handwriting in the undone seems of a manuscript.
I think I heard one of them say:
"the fire has burned out, there's only ashes left –
permanent as those stains on the sheets."

later downstairs in the bar bottles on the shelves behind the counter
like the silhouette of a city, seen during sunrise from the opposite shore.
just where was that and when? everything that is comes
like a voice from a receiver, which is thrown down hanging by the cord,
she asks "is this the end? or are we lost here
like those dusty western landscapes deep in their frames?"

is this the end?

At a Fast Food Restaurant

A girl with a backpack, in the shape of a bear,
despises time.

As if time
were like a roller coaster,
which pulls her forward,
and she has to labour with all her might,
so she doesn't start screaming
and covering her eyes with her hands.

She doesn't try to hurry
with the Happy Meal her father bought her –
a burger and fries,
those forbidden treasures,
scattered in front of her
all golden and enticing.

Their smell alone
would fill her mother with horror,
who counts kilograms,
like they count bodies after a catastrophe,
and tries the latest diet
to be more attractive to her new boyfriend
who sneers at her daughter
behind her back.

And she doesn't suck the last
of her pop loudly through the straw
so her father doesn't get annoyed,
who comes to visit her once a month,
so he can fulfill his duties
with an hour or two.

But what does it help,
if soon after he says
that it's time to take her home,
looking anxiously at the three narrow arrows
on his wristwatch –
his holy trinity –
God the Father, God the Son
and the Holy Spirit,
among which there is no place
for a daughter.

Scenes from a Juvenile Detention Centre

With the back of his head towards the camera.

He says that he wants to return to his life.
After this. When this is all over.
When he will have gotten used to
his own face again.

A view of their sleeping quarters.
Bunk beds.
It could be barracks or a dormitory.
If the keys on the keyring didn't jingle
louder than the siren of the police van.

And at night the lights are turned off
so they can learn to see
their own rage.

Lights out. They're sleeping,
they've put their slippers next to the bed –
a stone put in each one
so they don't fly off anywhere.

But this all remains off-screen.

Meanwhile we have already returned
to our comfortable, well-ordered lives,
where a door means an exit
and they don't have faces.

Next To

Will they sleep next to one another tonight?
Will they sleep next to one another after what happened,
after someone opened a door between them
to this crosswind, to this worry
and hammered a nail where there once had been a screw?
Will they sleep next to one another tonight?

Will they sleep next to one another, knowing
that now each has their own insomnia
and each their own alarm that will ring in the morning,
and a river in the middle, wrinkled waves, the sludge moves
towards the future, where the things they have collected together
might very well be sold at a garage sale, and the blanket will be
   too small?

And after waking up in the morning will they sit
at one table, not raising their eyes from their plates
so their glances don't meet, so they wouldn't see
the uncertainty, which is framed by their lit-up window?
And, when the glass that has fallen on the floor shatters,
how will they know – that it was for luck or misfortune?

Will they sleep next to one another
like scale pans, lingering doubt?
And, turned too tightly, the screws of years will break,
and in a dream she will fold the dried laundry
and put them in two separate baskets –
one for her clothes and one for his.

Someone has opened the door between them,
and a crosswind is blowing, and the blanket is too small,
the table, from which the glass will fall, is too narrow,
and the screws of years are turned too tightly,
but tonight they will sleep next to one another,
but tonight they will still sleep next to one another.

Commentary: Mandelstam

'We do not fly; we ascend only such towers as we ourselves are able to build.'
– Osip Mandelstam, The Morning of Acmeism

He put on a fur coat.
A demonstration flooded the streets – thousands of heads but
 not one face.
The fur coat fluffed up its feathers, as word moths hid in its
 lining and laid their eggs.

A stolen pencil stub. Which he worked with like a money
 counterfeiter.

Like Shakespeare's father, his father was a glove maker, but he
 examined pieces of ice
from the Neva with his bare hands.
That day the chill found its way into his blood.

A fish rots from the head.
A moustached man in a uniform tilts his head, from which
 terror had already poured over
half a continent.
He dedicated an anti-government poem to him. The addressee
 felt honoured.

That day he hid a razor in the sole of his boot. Or was it a key?
 A horseshoe?

The fear grew and crawled around – ants, looking for a path
 in the pipes and ducts so they could eavesdrop in on the
 conversations.

He was interrogated once again.
The typewriter rattled away, it had numerous keyboards and
 pedals like an organ.
Someone with rolled-up sleeves pounded the keys, sunk up to his
 elbows in the machine's
heavy mass.

It wasn't a protocol. It was a phone bill for calls to the dead –
five years in a corrective labour camp.

He didn't hold out. The cold had already advanced too far.

The tower was finished.
In his dream he climbed up it and looked at the snow-blanketed
 expanse.
Someone had come quietly from behind
and pushed him.

For many years the suitcase with manuscripts hid under the bed
 and grew fins.
It was sentenced for even longer than its owner.
Sometimes someone closed the door behind himself and opened it,
and its scales gave off a glow like a television screen,
illuminating the darker side of his posthumous biography.

D

****
———

To climb down to the sea
between rocks with hunched backs.
They are dark, as if they had been tanned in the miserly sun.
There are also large, jagged broken-off pieces from the cliff,
which the waves have made docile as the cornerstones of manor houses.

Each rock, even the finest of them, is like a small altar.
Rocks have deep roots,
ruins in particular.
Deeper than people have.

To lift a pebble, flat as
the earth,
if you believe Hesiod.
To warm it in your palm,
and afterwards put it back in its place.
And what would you need it for?
One doesn't come back from those same places the same as they were before anyway.
And nothing is allowed to be taken from here
and nothing is allowed to be left –
after smoking you put the used match back in the matchbox.
Soon there won't be anything in your pockets that hasn't been touched by fire.

You've given your body and clothing to metal detectors more than once,
your luggage – to the x-ray machine,
and now you don't have anything that could be sharp, or you could cut with, inflict with pain.
Nothing dangerous – neither weapons, nor scissors, not even a lighter.

(The ancients believed that iron tools, especially those that were sharp,
protected one from evil spirits, curses, disease.
Now there are sleeping pills, aspirin, antibiotics.
And you can buy bread and meat that's sliced up already.
What gave the ancients a sense of security
terrifies us.)

We have banished the demons to the sewer pipes
and madness,
only the strongest among them
have stayed in our dreams.

You already wanted to write it down on the plane,
but the pen started to leak –
at that height it isn't possible to write
what you have to think about here, close to the earth.
Looking from there, even pain doesn't have names,
just numbers – like avenues in a big city.

There are just headlines above –
here, below – twisted metal, broken glass.
The waves crash against bare rocks
without air bags,
life jackets.
The sea is also on its way.
Its surface rises like a chest when someone out of breath gasps for air.
(Here you have to smoke so you don't forget you need to breathe.)

Waves
crumpled up like clothes in a backpack packed in a hurry before escaping.

Back to the manor.

There you have to sleep in a heavy ebony bed
that has a longer history than a majority of the homes,
where you have come from.

A bed with roots.

It's decorated with scenes from the Bible.
The fall from sin. The manger in Bethlehem. The flight from
 Egypt.
Brief images. Stills again. Snapshots.

Celtic patterns on a rug,
ornaments, which get lost on the way to a non-existing centre.
They had replicated them from the sea.

Shrunken into a ball,
you sink deep into slumber like a cornerstone into the ground,
as your thoughts
wander through the empty floors of the house there up above.

from The End of Summer and Other Poems

9.

Your head found peace in my hands
like a bird that sleeps on the ground.
We are from this world.

We wanted to be a mirror
that reflects everything, leaves nothing inside itself,
but life flowed through us
like light through curtains,
awakening someone peacefully –
right when their dream is over. We are from this
world.

We are open like
a door that opens inward.
We are from this world.

10.

The salespeople were taking the necklaces from the velvet necks
in the jewellery stores' display windows.

The postage stamp with a bird that was in the drawer
had already started forgetting
about its flight via airmail.

We examined each other
carefully like customs control
or a doctor looking for vulnerable spots:
"Does this hurt? And here?"

My caresses were gloves,
I could touch you with:
"Is this good? And here?"

After we had slept naked together,
we got dressed again,
but the love still stayed inside us.

Like when they put stitches in a wound,
but the pain remains.

Forgetting

The pawn shop, where we sold your rings,
was shuttered.
The silver spoons that you got for your baptism
have disappeared.

Oblivion smells like disinfectant.
We scattered salt on the floor
and our memories
and poured chlorine – on our history.

We buried you so deep,
but you
still come to us in our dreams
and don't say a word.

Spring

It was a warm day, and for the first time this year I wore a light coat. And I found a strip of
paper, which was lying in my pocket forgotten for the whole winter.
A few random words, written down on a rainy day, crumbled in my fingers like damp match heads against a matchbox strip. When was that? How long ago was that?
A few cold months, the crooked wall calendar. Enough days to lose count of them– crumbs, which we have gathered from under the funeral reception table.
It seemed to me that something had happened to your photos – I examined them long
and hard and – no memory of it at all. I didn't even know if that's you there. As if in each photo you were looking past the camera lens.
But then – a few indecipherable scribbles and I remember everything.

It was a warm day, and I wore a light coat, but I – was cold.

Washing Father

He scrubs his father's back.
His father doesn't understand anything
and doesn't reply when others
call his name.

He is too deep
in his body's wrinkles and folds,
too deep for him
to come out of.

Once he awoke in an unknown place.
He put on his glasses.
The lenses steamed up
from what he saw
and his nose began to bleed.

When he returned,
he refused to talk,
forgetting everything
that he had acquired over the years.

His windpipe froze over,
and the circulating blood is still
fighting in vain
to thaw it.

His heartbeats –
they are tracks in the snow
beyond the polar circle.
The wind erases them.

Only the wrinkles
on his skin
are deep – deep
like surgical scars.

Time has left gashes all over his body
like an unskilled surgeon,
who couldn't save anyone,
but just cut and cut, and cut.

He doesn't talk.
His hair grows,
his nails grow,
but he doesn't understand anything.

With a rough towel
he dries his father's body –
a soft towel is of no use to anyone,
a soft towel doesn't absorb moisture.

When he shaves his father's beard,
his father sits in front of him, just
like old times, as he sat in front of
the mirror while shaving himself.

He puts on his father's suitcoat.
It seems too big.
His father shrinks
a few sizes a year.

The suitcoat's pockets are empty
like his father's memory,
its buttons are as dull
as his father's gaze.

He combs his father's hair
and ties his shoes.
He places his father
where the man of the house sits – at the end of the table.

His father doesn't understand anything,
his dominion an arid field,
and he – his son – humbly nurses
that withering legacy of his.

From a Distance

I was driven, propped up like a stiff figure,
along low trees that had opened up their foliage of electric light.
I sent thoughts to myself to the future:
there's not a person on the street – everyone's dissolved into
    reality like the outlines of a face in a dark room.

I am wrapped up in blankets, but inside me everything is
    burning –
a flame that's built up strength could cast a second into a bullet.
it's the the beginning of the nineties, the motor of a Moskvitch
    roars.
a fever has come over it as well and it's shaking and shivering.

at that moment I shoot an arrow.
its trajectory looms throughout the years.
it's finally reached me, this morning before the dawn:

a coin laying in a floor crack, awaiting to be found,
a note is crumpled up into a ball, passed from pupil to pupil
    under the benches so the teacher doesn't see it,
having travelled eighteen years to its addressee.

Brother

You were four when they told you
"This is your brother."
They didn't explain anything more,
they simply said:
"This is your brother."

You were curious
and gradually suspicion was born in you.

I followed your footsteps,
everywhere I went you were already in front of me.
The door handle was still warm
as I grasped it in my palm.

And who always sat
in the front seat of the car next to dad –
at the right hand of our father?

You hid me.
Everyone was supposed to think that you're the only one.
How could anyone believe in your powers,
if there's this double
behind your back?

You were afraid that I'd take away your scent
and no one would recognize you anymore.

I stood behind your back
in your old sweater,
my shoes, the laces of which
always came untied.

I stood behind your back
putting stones in my pockets
so the world would finally feel
my weight.

I observed and I studied
I was not yet ready
And I alone developed my abilities
polishing each vertebra,
each joint
that I acquired, standing in the shadows
and waiting,
until you
would not need them anymore.

The sawdust spilled on the ground.
I worked like a patient artisan
while putting myself together.
Sometimes you wanted to drive those stubborn sprouts
right back into me,
the ones, mimicking you,
that mocked you.
You thought they were weapons
which threatened you.

"You can't do that," they told you
"That's your brother."
But you didn't believe them.
Being a brother was a task
that I still needed to fulfill.

And I waited.
I observed and I studied.
On the tips of my toes,
I strove to look over your shoulder.

The years worked to my advantage,
And then, one day, I came into the light.

I had acquired the family scent
and I carried the family traits on my face.

The sun was shining, but that didn't bother me.
I finally had a shadow, still I had to break it in.
I was not yet perfect, still I was myself.

"This is my brother," you said,
"This is my brother."

Commentary: Johannes Bobrowski

The grass is stretched out in all its height.
A column of smoke rises straight up,
measuring the low-lying clouds.

In the orchard
the green branches
are tangled up with those that are withered –
life lines and death lines.

The foliage frees itself from the ballast.
The hollow steps of the apples ring out.

Darkness comes,
a forest creature follows its tracks,
looking for fallen fruit.

The flight of a bird –
dark and mute lightning –
slowly flashes across the sky.

He was here
and saw it.

Language opened eyes
like someone who awakens in the night
from his own screaming.

What merciless lowlands!
What an unbearable forgiveness!

Commentary: July 16th, 2011

On an outing with our bikes I sped past the others. I pedaled as fast as my strength
allowed, fleeing like a splinter from the blast's epicentre.
I left the city behind me and the sheet of paper on the table with that day's date instead of a title.
And nothing more.
The paper's white emptiness grew. It seemed I was in a hurry, so it wouldn't find me. It was like he, who had died that morning in another city, was around close by somewhere and was pursuing me.
He, who could live, if not for his wrist watch, the hands of which had already started turning deathwise, hurrying years ahead of time.
There is a compass somewhere that hesitates. The magnetic needle makes a circle. It flashes like the spokes of a wheel. Every once in a while it stops for a moment – a roulette ball, which doesn't indicate the winner, but the one that lost.
I glanced back. Down the hill I let my bike slide idly through the forest shadows.
The white splotch of the page continued to grow behind me, the unwritten swelled and expanded, filling up space after space like gas, searching for me.
Suddenly I turned off the road. I stopped on the roadside and waited.

Lightning Source UK Ltd.
Milton Keynes UK
UKHW040623250620
365522UK00005B/342